THE LITTLE
INSTRUCTION
BOOK FOR
RETIREMENT

THE LITTLE INSTRUCTION BOOK FOR RETIREMENT

Illustrations by Ian Baker

An Hachette UK Company
www.hachette.co.uk

Summersdale Publishers Ltd
Part of Octopus Publishing Group Limited
Carmelite House
50 Victoria Embankment
LONDON
EC4Y 0DZ
UK

www.summersdale.com

Printed and bound in China

ISBN: 978-1-78783-572-6

THE LITTLE
INSTRUCTION
BOOK FOR
RETIREMENT

KATE FREEMAN

ILLUSTRATIONS BY IAN BAKER

summersdale

Working people have
a lot of bad habits, but
the worst of them is work.

CLARENCE DARROW

INTRODUCTION

Ah, the joys of being retired! From here on out it's all lazy lie-ins, pleasant afternoons in the garden (or the garden centre) and evenings spent in a comfy chair in front of the fire, right? Wrong! Welcome to a world where you're halfway to the office before you realize you don't work there any more, you somehow have even less free time than you did before and suddenly daytime TV is a whole lot more appealing than it ever used to be…

But don't panic! Help is at hand in the form of this little instruction book, which will guide you safely through the pitfalls and pleasures of being retired and, most importantly, teach you how to make sure you always get a decent afternoon nap. Enjoy!

INSTRUCTION NO.1

IT'S TIME TO CELEBRATE THE
END OF AN ERA – AND THE START
OF A WHOLE NEW ONE!

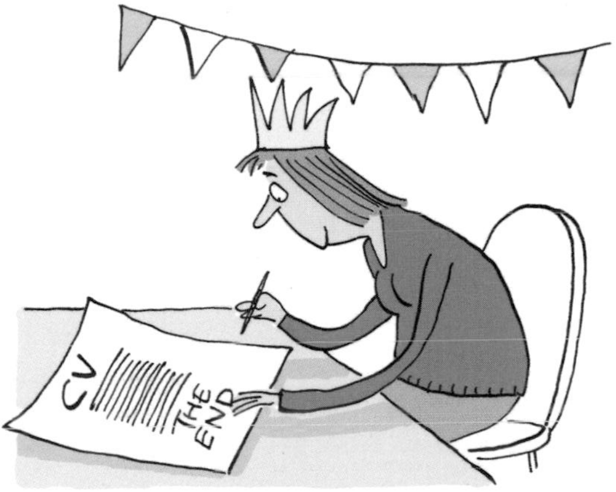

CV
THE END

YOU NOW FINALLY HAVE ALL THE FREE TIME IN THE WORLD TO DEDICATE TO NEW HOBBIES, LEARNING A NEW LANGUAGE, READING ALL THE WORTHY BOOKS YOU ALWAYS ASSUMED YOU'D GET TO ONE DAY AND VOLUNTEERING FOR GOOD CAUSES.

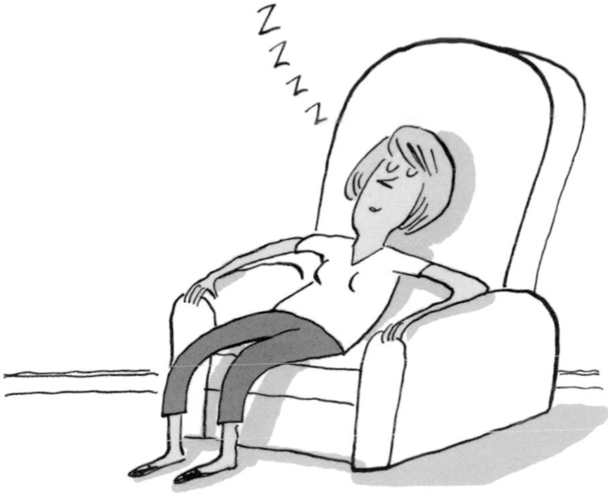
ZZZZ

SMOOTH THE TRANSITION
FROM WORKING LIFE TO RETIREMENT
BY HOLDING A "MORNING MEETING"
EVERY DAY TO BRIEF THE HOUSEHOLD
ON THE DAY'S EVENTS.

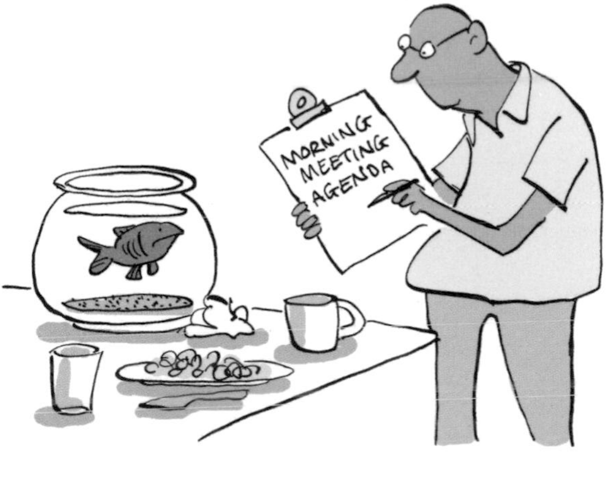
MORNING
MEETING
AGENDA

INSTRUCTION NO.4

DAYS OF THE WEEK NOW HAVE NO
BEARING ON YOUR LIFE WHATSOEVER –
EVERY DAY IS THE WEEKEND!

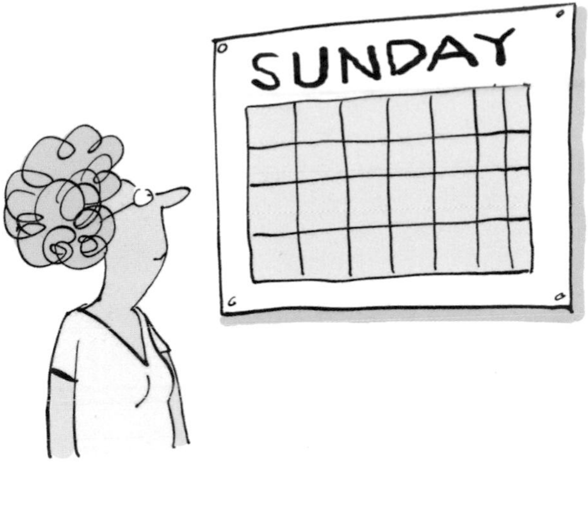
SUNDAY

NEVER DRINK COFFEE AFTER MIDDAY –
IT'LL KEEP YOU UP ALL AFTERNOON.

RETIREMENT CAN BE CONFUSING AND HARD TO GET USED TO AT FIRST. WHEN IN DOUBT, GO TO THE GARDEN CENTRE.

YOU MUST NOW MAKE HOUSEHOLD CHORES
TAKE AT LEAST THREE TIMES LONGER
THAN WHEN YOU WERE HOLDING DOWN A
FULL-TIME JOB, JUST TO FILL SOME TIME.

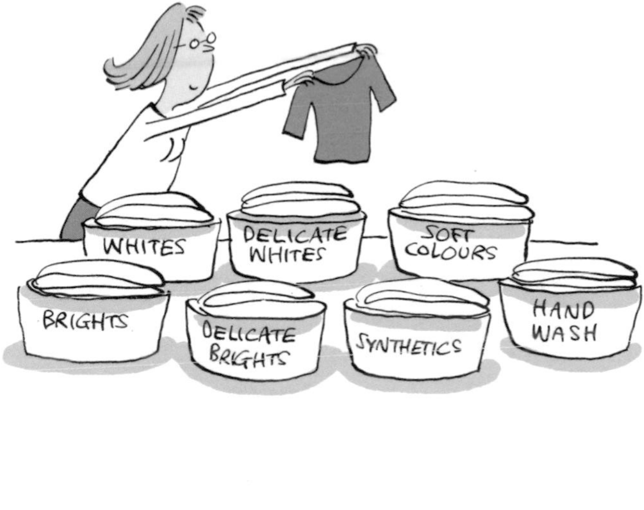
WHITES
DELICATE WHITES
SOFT COLOURS
BRIGHTS
DELICATE BRIGHTS
SYNTHETICS
HAND WASH

YOU MAY START TO MISS HAVING LOTS OF DAILY INTERACTIONS WITH OTHER HUMANS, BUT THIS ISN'T AN EXCUSE TO TALK THE EAR OFF ANYONE WHO COMES TO THE FRONT DOOR.

WHILE THERE'S NO LONGER ANY
NEED TO DRESS SMARTLY EVERY DAY,
YOU SHOULD PROBABLY STILL GET
DRESSED, AT LEAST SOMETIMES.

IF YOU MISS BEING AT WORK BUT YOU
DON'T WANT TO ADMIT IT, YOU CAN BECOME
A PILLAR OF YOUR LOCAL COMMUNITY.
COMMITTEE MEETINGS, HERE YOU COME!

THIS IS A NEW CHAPTER IN YOUR LIFE,
SO IT'S TIME TO TRY NEW THINGS!

SET YOUR ALARM CLOCK FOR 6 A.M.
PURELY FOR THE JOY OF TURNING IT
OFF AND SLEEPING LONGER.

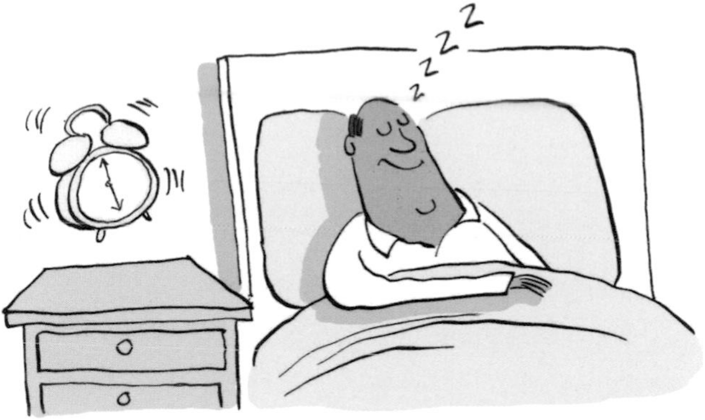
z z Z Z

YOUR NUMBER-ONE CHOICE OF FOOTWEAR
WILL PROBABLY NOW BE SLIPPERS,
SO MAKE SURE YOU'RE PREPARED.

YOUR RETIREMENT IS THE
PERFECT TIME TO GET STARTED
ON THAT BUCKET LIST.

AFTER YEARS OF SEEING EACH OTHER ONLY BRIEFLY, YOU CAN NOW FINALLY GET TO KNOW YOUR PARTNER, AS YOU HAVE PLENTY OF UNBROKEN TIME TO SPEND TOGETHER.

FINALLY, IT'S YOUR TIME TO DRIVE IN RUSH
HOUR WHEN YOU DON'T REALLY NEED TO.

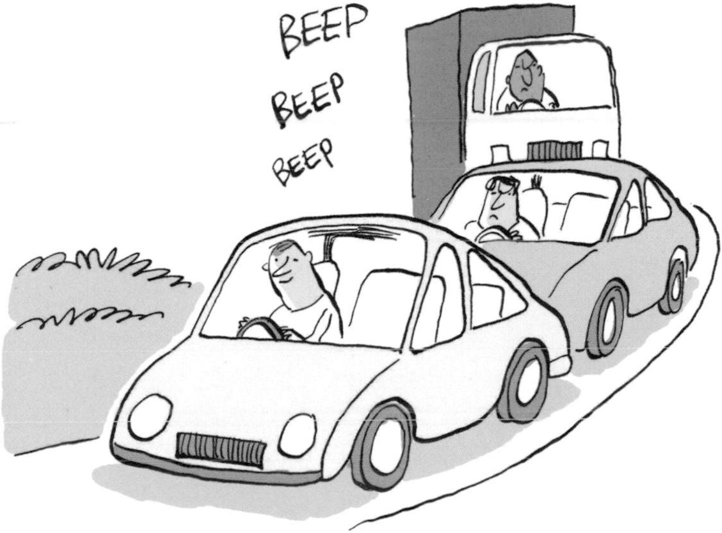
BEEP
BEEP
BEEP

INVEST IN A COMPANION. A DOG,
A CAT, A HAMSTER, A SNAKE, A PARROT...
THE MORE, THE MERRIER!

NOW YOU HAVE TIME TO TAKE
UP ALL THE HOBBIES!

WHO SAID NETFLIX WAS JUST FOR
YOUNGSTERS TO BINGE? YOU NOW HAVE
MORE TIME ON YOUR HANDS THAN THEM!

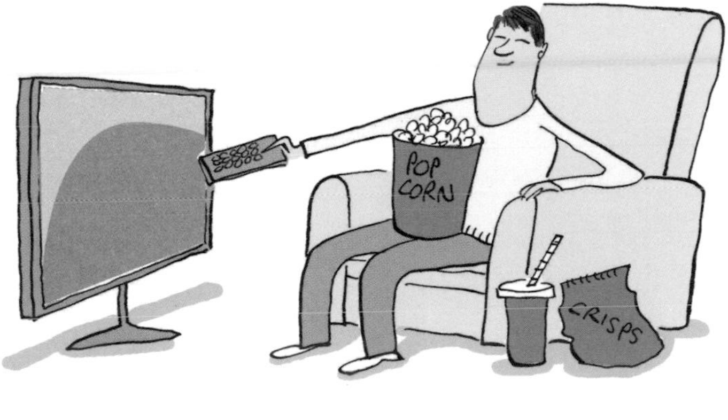
POP
CORN
CRISPS

INSTRUCTION NO.20

ENJOY KNOWING THAT YOU
CAN DO HOME IMPROVEMENTS
WHENEVER YOU FEEL LIKE IT.

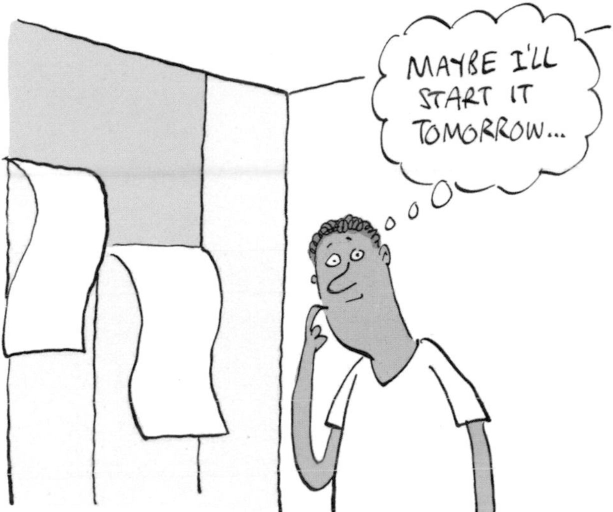
MAYBE I'LL START IT TOMORROW...

WHEN YOU GREW UP, YOU PUT AWAY
CHILDISH THINGS. FRANKLY, IT'S WAY
PAST TIME TO GET THEM OUT AGAIN.

INSTRUCTION NO.22

THERE'S ABSOLUTELY NOTHING
A HOT DRINK AND A NICE
SIT-DOWN CAN'T FIX.

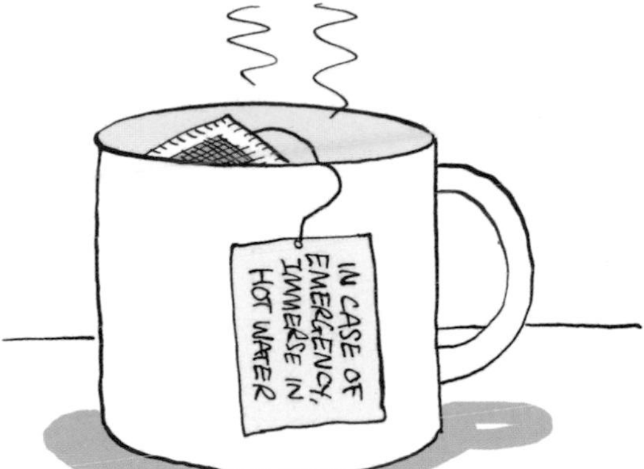
IN CASE OF
EMERGENCY,
IMMERSE IN
HOT WATER

INSTRUCTION NO.23

RETIREMENT IS ALL ABOUT ENJOYING
YOURSELF, SO PUSH THE BOAT OUT.
PUSH THE WHOLE DAMN FLEET OUT.

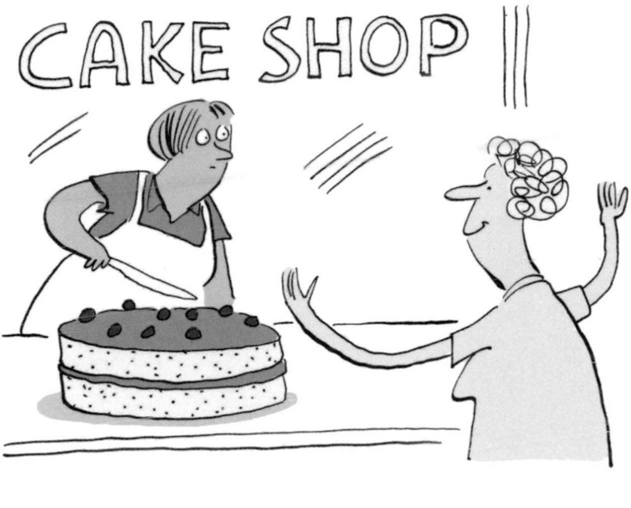
CAKE SHOP

THE GREYER YOUR HAIR AND THE LONGER
YOUR BEARD, THE MORE LIKELY PEOPLE
ARE TO BELIEVE YOU'RE A WISE OLD SAGE.
CONSIDER STARTING YOUR OWN CULT.

ALL THOSE CLASSICS YOU NEVER GOT ROUND
TO READING? NO EXCUSES NOW! TACKLE
THOSE VERBOSE RUSSIANS FOR STARTERS.

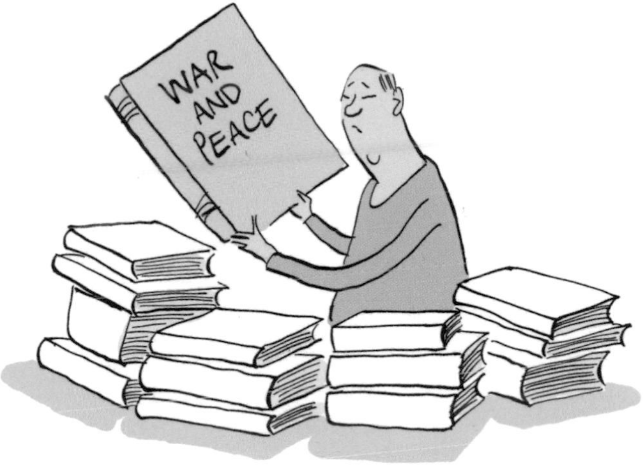
WAR
AND
PEACE

YOU'LL NEED TO FIND ANY EXCUSE TO LEAVE THE HOUSE NOW, JUST SO YOU CAN RETURN TO A HERO'S WELCOME FROM YOUR FOUR-LEGGED FRIEND.

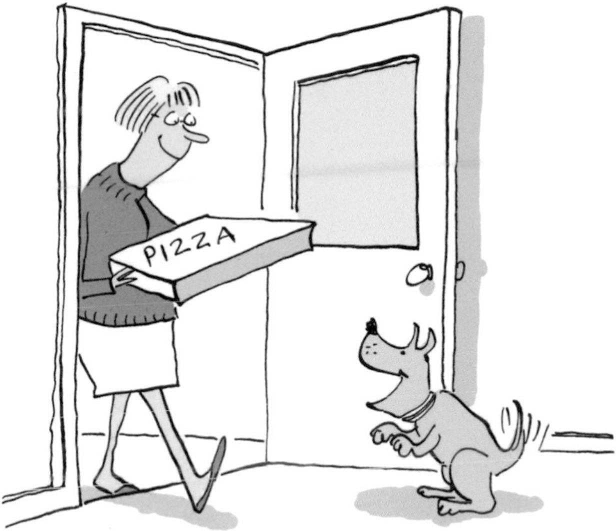
PIZZA

LIVE EVERY DAY AS IF IT WERE YOUR LAST.
SEE EACH MOMENT AS AN OPPORTUNITY
TO BLOW YOUR KIDS' INHERITANCE.

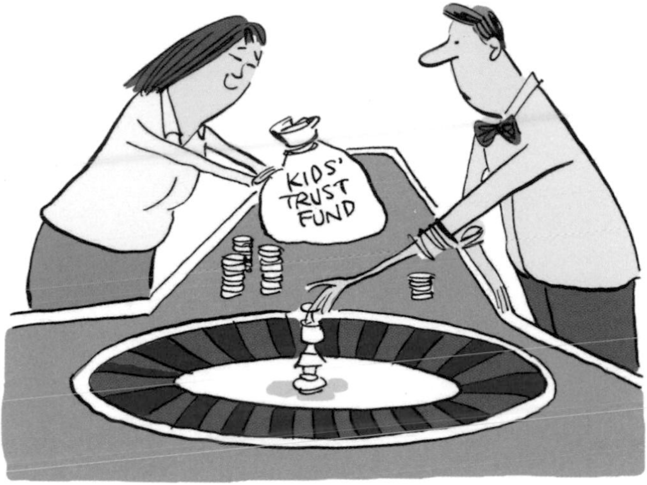
KIDS'
TRUST
FUND

DON'T MAKE THE MISTAKE OF BEING
RELIABLE — YOU'LL ONLY END UP
BEING THE UNPAID BABYSITTER
FOR YOUR GRANDKIDS!

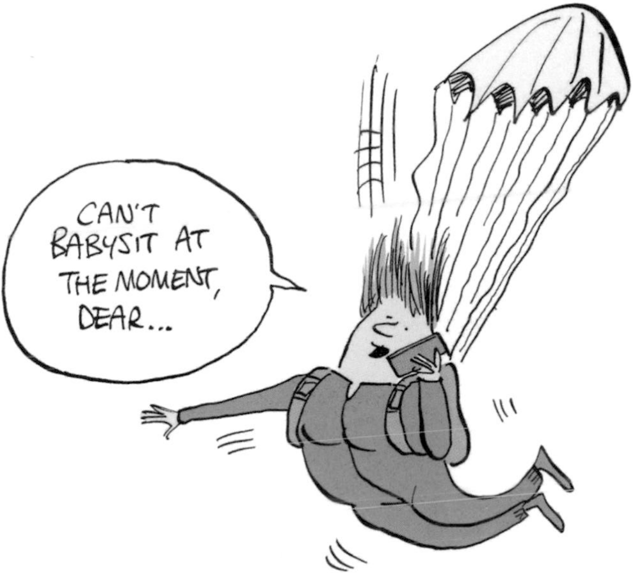
CAN'T BABYSIT AT THE MOMENT, DEAR...

FLOG OFF ALL THOSE ITEMS YOU
DEFINITELY WON'T BE NEEDING
IN YOUR LIFE ANY MORE.

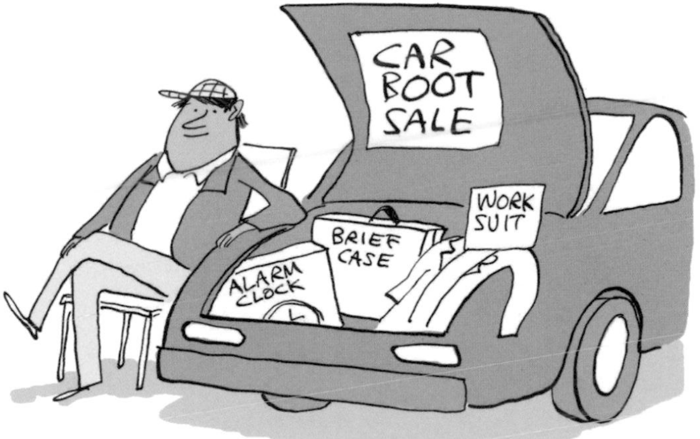
CAR BOOT SALE
WORK SUIT
BRIEF CASE
ALARM CLOCK

ENJOY THE FACT THAT YOU NO LONGER HAVE ONLY AN HOUR FOR LUNCH BY CREATING A GOURMET SEVEN-COURSE MEAL THAT STRETCHES FROM JUST AFTER YOUR MORNING COFFEE RIGHT UP TO DINNER TIME.

NOW YOU CAN CONCENTRATE ON
YOUR ROLE AS HEAD OF THE FAMILY
AND MEDDLE AT WILL. IT'S THE
MOST FUN YOU'LL EVER HAVE.

KEEP THOSE GREY CELLS IN
TIP-TOP CONDITION AND WORK YOUR
WAY THROUGH EVERY QUIZ BOOK
YOU CAN LAY YOUR HANDS ON. WHO
KNOWS? YOU MIGHT ENJOY A SECOND
CAREER AS A DAYTIME QUIZ CHAMP!

BEAT THE YOUTH

| 26 | 1,000,000 |
| SCORE | SCORE |

REMEMBER, YOU'LL ALWAYS BE YOUNGER THAN
CHER AND SHE'S NOT SLOWING DOWN ANY
TIME SOON, SO WHY SHOULD YOU?

INSTRUCTION NO.34

NOW YOU CAN SPEND SO MUCH MORE
TIME WITH THE ONES YOU LOVE.

REMEMBER: THERE'S NOTHING
TO BE STRESSED ABOUT ANY MORE.
WELL, APART FROM JIGSAW PUZZLES.

NOW YOU'RE LIVING OFF YOUR MEASLY
PENSION, YOU MAY HAVE TO FIND
OTHER SOURCES OF INCOME.

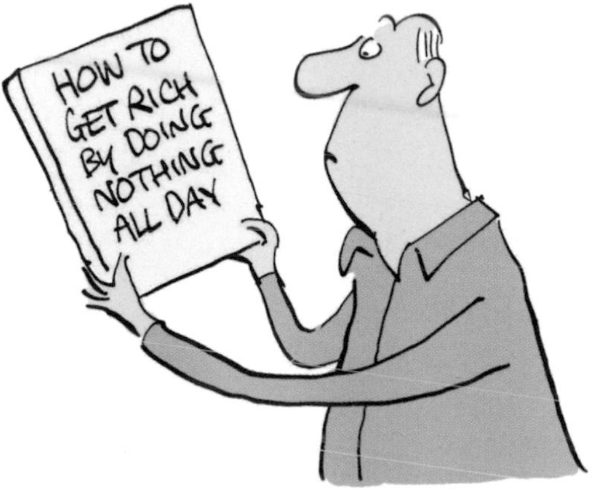
HOW TO GET RICH BY DOING NOTHING ALL DAY

OF COURSE, THERE MIGHT BE
TIMES WHEN RETIREMENT STILL
REQUIRES HARD WORK.

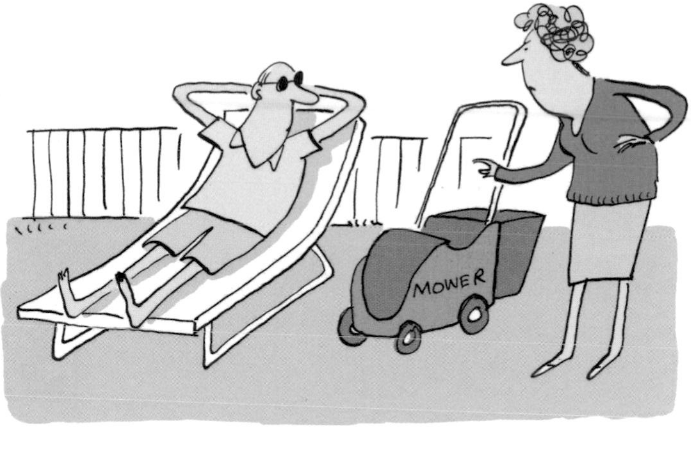
MOWER

NOW THAT YOU NO LONGER HAVE TO GET UP
FOR WORK AT AN UNGODLY HOUR, YOU CAN
STAY UP AS LONG AS YOU WANT!

MAKE THE MOST OF THE FREE TRAVEL AND
MAKE NEW FRIENDS AT THE SAME TIME BY
STAYING ON THE BUS FOR THE ENTIRE ROUTE,
ENTERTAINING EVERYONE WHO GETS ON
WITH THE STORY OF YOUR LIFE.

RETIREMENT IS A GREAT OPPORTUNITY
TO CONSIDER RELOCATING.

MAKE SURE YOU FIND A SUITABLE OUTLET
FOR COMPLAINING ABOUT YOUR STRUGGLE
TO FILL ALL THE FREE TIME YOU HAVE.

INSTRUCTION NO.42

TAKE UP AN OUTDOOR HOBBY,
SUCH AS BIRDWATCHING.

NOW IS THE TIME TO GET TO
GRIPS WITH ALL OF THOSE JOBS
YOU'VE BEEN PUTTING OFF.

BRING YOUR LOOK IN LINE WITH YOUR
NEW, STRESS-FREE SET-UP.

USE SOME OF YOUR TIME TO VISIT THE
PLACES YOU'VE ALWAYS WANTED TO GO.

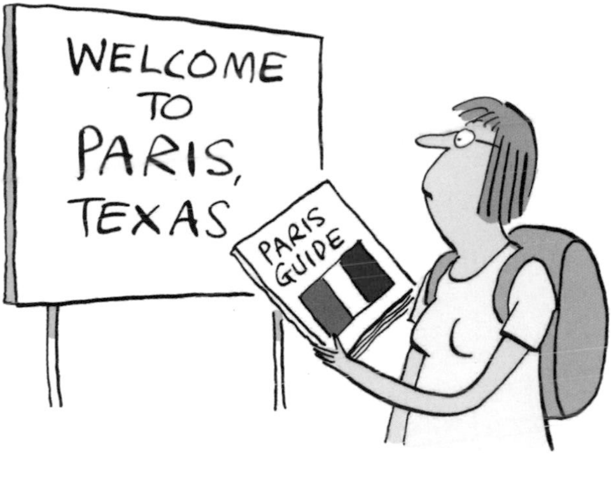
WELCOME
TO
PARIS,
TEXAS
PARIS
GUIDE

IF YOU'RE INTERESTED IN FINDING OUT MORE
ABOUT OUR BOOKS, FIND US ON FACEBOOK AT
SUMMERSDALE PUBLISHERS AND FOLLOW US
ON TWITTER AT @SUMMERSDALE.

WWW.SUMMERSDALE.COM